The Braeland Poems

The Braeland Poems

Soliloquies

Michael Ryle

WESTBRAE LITERARY GROUP

ISBN: 979-8-9917199-4-0
Published by Westbrae Literary Group
Berkeley, California
Jon-David Hague, Founding Editor

For more information about this and other titles from Westbrae Literary Group, visit us at westbraeliterarygroup.com or email us at info@westbraeliterarygroup.com

For my wife, Beverly, who makes all good things happen

CONTENTS

Twenty Soliloquies

The Women

Blank verse,
it hardly seems
like verse at all sometimes,
more like a favorite worn-out pair
of shoes.

Twenty Soliloquies

i. (after Sappho poem 1)

She's been to the finest spas, around the world—
Dubai, for the placenta facials,
Hong Kong, for ultrasonic collagen,
hammams and Vichy showers in Marrakech,
Himalayan abhyanga oil massage,
microneedle wands of foreskin stem cells,
blood platelets, bee venom, goldleaf—

Yet, in a pinch, I'm the one she calls.

"Come to me, Vaness," her message says,
"or you'll crush my spirit like a petal.
If ever I could count on you before,
I need you now. I'm in an awful place—
my cave drips with pain."

                    That's my Dora,
drama queen, without a doubt. But still,
my best client, been with me forever.
Mother, sister, best friend, I'm a little
of all three to her.

                    "The tour from Hell
ends tonight in Milan," she writes,
"and after that I never want to sing
a note or finger a guitar again.
Even now, as I tap these words,
my chariot with flocks of sparrows painted
on the wings jets the ocean toward

the Evening Star on its way to you.
Your private cabin's filled with fresh-cut flowers,
silken pillows, finest linens, stars
stippled on the ceiling. My limousine
will be waiting for you at the airport.
We'll go shopping at La Galleria,
run like children through the Liberty Fountain,
go to Brera, snicker at *Il Bacio,*
sprawl out on the terrace while the brook
whispers gossip through the apple blossoms.
I know I ask a lot for you to drop
what you're doing now and come to me,
but if I have you here, you possessing
everything and knowing everything,
I know I cannot fail."

                  Oh, my goodness,
dearest Dora, what's the matter now?
What absconded lover must I restore
to your arms, *this* time? What goes on
in that crazy, crazy heart of yours?

She falls and every time she's off and running
like a filly in a springtime meadow.
A lovely face, a coy look withdrawn,
her joints melt, her heart palpitates,
her eyes shellac, her ears jangle, the sweat
pours, she's wet as the morning dew.

She loves as if love's the only thing
on earth, the careless ones who treat her worst

and leave her grasping after with her spirit
like an oak hammered by the wind,
a monster with a hundred waving arms.

Whoever's wronged her now, I suspect
it's someone younger. Dora's not so old
herself, but she feels it, and she thinks
that I have swindles up my sleeve to make
the girl relent, that I can soften her
like the callus on a foot, and if
she's not in love, she will be when I'm done.

Well, skin I know, and hair and nails, and scrubs,
massage, meditation, mindfulness,
nutrition, circulation, general wellness,
all the paths to the happy hormones.
If this buys her a night of feeling
loved, the money is well-spent, I think.

Yet the truth is, all you have to do
is bind her balayage in a purple
headband, sit her down with her guitar
and listen to her sing her songs, and you
will think, here's someone who's found a purl
in time, who'll never grow a moment older.

Dora, dearest love, of course I'll come.

ii.

How you doing, guys, it's great to be—
who am I? Sorry, I forgot
to say my name. I'm Linda, Linda B.
Three Lindas here tonight—big ass meeting.

What am I? You almost got me there.
I can't say the word, not just yet.
I'm holding at step zero, crossing off
the days, one drip at a time. Ninety
means I'm done, I can go, right?
Come on guys, laugh—that was funny.

My sponsor says I gotta claim my seat,
get off my ass and share. So here I am,
sharing now, but don't expect the skinny,
the chapter and verse of my insanity.

You guys know my story, anyway—
the shit did such a job of covering up
the pain, I didn't notice it become
the pain, bit by bit, usurping me,
until my friends, the ones I used to have,
now they're all asking, where the fuck is Linda?

I might breathe free a day, a week, a month,
but one thing always led to another,
back down in the hole with the shovel.

And then I wind up here—what the fuck?
Somebody tell me how. Anybody.
By the grace of you-know-who, you say.

I'm confused, I say. That's good, you say—
confusion is the first stage of knowledge.

My demons knock me over at a touch.
There's no music on my radio,
just the same commercial, back-to-back—
What you want with Mr Prettygood
when Billy Paradise is on the line?

This too shall pass, you say—that's your response.
Put down the baseball bat and we'll talk,
get off the fucking cross, we need the wood,
save face or save your ass, not both,
coming here's the easy way out,
when all else fails, do what they say,
slow down, patience takes patience,
your head's a bad neighborhood at night.

You guys got one for every circumstance.
You crack me up, I laugh my ass off,
beats the television, Thursday nights.

I could go on, but hey, enough's enough.
This sharing's maybe not so bad—might try
it again. You guys may wish you never
got me started. Thanks for glistening.

iii.

Idris coming to the last eight,
cuts his eyes across at me.
My solo's next.

Tap the valves so they're nice and loose,
breathe warm air into the horn
and shake the condensation out,
sip of Stoli for the cottonmouth.

Idris double-timing now—
cat's a goddam circular-breathing force of nature.
Pick up the line where he leaves off,
step on his last note with your first
so trumpet follows sax, seamlessly,
and they won't know where Idris ends and I begin.

But hell, they don't, anyway,
no more than they can tell a bass from a cello,
a soprano sax from a clarinet.

Silence, that'll grab 'em by the ass.
Step into the light,
put the horn to your mouth,
and—nothing.
Leave the first bar open,
then the second,
the way a two-strike hitter lets the pitch go by.
Make 'em wonder while the piano fills,

then two more beats of rest
and restate the tune,
displaced,
softly with the Harmon mute
like Miles.
Monk says fuck the changes, solo on the melody.
Glide from note to note
like Lady Day,
half-valve gliss,
then pull the mute and double-time the turnaround
just to show the motherfuckers you can.

Femme at table four is digging on the music, I can tell—
her boyfriend, not so much.
Maybe just her date.
If she was mine,
I wouldn't sit way over there—
snuggle up with her.

Get to the bridge,
D-flat's a lyrical key,
get lyrical,
woo her with the horn,
how Chet Baker got more pussy than Ray Charles.
Nice to think about, but unlikely—
she's desitively Upper West Side.

But hey, Nicky was too,
and in she walks one night with this Wall Street type,
leaves with me.

The memory is like this tune,
one I haven't played for so long
I forgot how good it is.
We had some times.

Get the women out your head,
your mind back on the music.
Two more bars, you're in.

Forget the silence,
announce yourself,
high C
and take it higher,
just like Roy.

Shades on,
step out of the shadows like the stranger in an old movie,
burn the motherfucker,
here we go.

iv.

Plan A, I creep up from behind, and with
the barrel one inch from the tender spot
below the occipital protuberance,
I fire. At such close range it's hard to miss.

Quicker than the sonofabitch deserves,
but clean, at least—the .22 lacks
sufficient mass and velocity
to go the distance to the frontal lobes
and exit in a spray of blood and bone.

Plan B is the garotte. Quick it ain't,
but there are other things to think about.
Besides the noxious fecal smell, there is
the likelihood I'd lose my nerve before
the hands let go, the arms began to twitch
and like a tower sapped from underneath,
the body wheeled and caved upon itself.

Poison is a possibility,
but kind, concentration, dosage—there's
a lot to know, a lot to go awry.

And so I go on planning A to Z,
not, "This I did," but, "suchlike would I do."
Is it conscience? No, the problem is,
I could only kill him once, and once
could never be enough to right the scales.

For true satisfaction I would need
the power to bid him rise, like Lazarus.

The second time, who knows, I might say, Hell,
go ahead, use piano wire,
just don't forget the clothespin for your nose.

Number three might be something new,
some lethal method of my own device.

But it would never work. He'd figure out
I couldn't leave him to oblivion.
A person can get used to anything
and even daily dying beats the void
that waits should I decline to bring him back.
He'd know he had me there and he'd laugh
and mock me to my face.

So it's best to leave things as they are.

v.

Down the left side of the little screen,
bubble messages like soldiers marching
in a line—the other side is empty,
no replies from me.

                     Her texts get shorter,
more insistent, less time in between.
What's going on with me? she demands.
Why the sudden disappearing act?
Am I ghosting her? (*smiley-face*)

I would reply, but at the moment, I'm
half drunk. A couple more, I'll be completely
drunk and I'll forget. Hit me again.

It's cold outside, thirty-, twenty-something.
I could drive around with all the windows
down until I sober up and go
knock on her door.

                   But then she'd speak and I
would listen for the other woman's voice,
she'd turn to me and I would look to see
the other woman's face. The last time I
saw Maeve I wished, God help me, she would vanish
in a puff of smoke and leave the other
woman standing in her place.

Back when, we were a pair of circus clowns,

catapulted from the cannons of
divorce, turning, tumbling in the air.
That first night, over cappuccino,
I meant to make it clear, a thousand miles
away from love was still too close for me,
but she went even further—*light years*, she said.

With that out of the way, there was no reason
for us not to fall in line. On Wednesdays,
I worked late and when she put her kids
to bed, I came by for a taste.
On Saturdays they were with their dad
and I stayed overnight.

                      Fixed, like clockwork,
carnal pleasure as it was intended,
pure and clean, untainted, undefiled
by sentiment and its attendant nightmares,
marriage minus wedlock, the silver nugget
at its center with the dross burned off.

Holidays we went our separate ways,
birthday cards were satirical,
anniversaries slipped by unnoticed.

We didn't read the same best-selling books,
sit by the fire, take evening walks,
go dancing, talk about the film we saw,
swap playlists, exercise or cook together.

We also didn't lie or cheat, get jealous,

whine with boredom, squabble over money,
chores, habits, relatives, perceived neglect,
or wish each other different than we were.

One day I ran into her shopping with
a friend and she pretended not to know me.
The friend took her arm, pulled her away,
and Maeve looked back at me and shook her head,
her finger to her lips. Later on,
she asked me if I minded and I laughed—
I was glad to be her backdoor man.

We had what we had, and without
the creeping fungus of romance, I
was sure that it would last.

                          That was before
the other woman came into the picture.

I had no experience with death—
it was alien to me. The night
Maeve phoned to say her father died, I was
as tongue-tied as a child caught in a lie.

She fell silent and I asked her if
she wanted me to come. "Oh, yes," she cried,
which I did not expect.

                          Despite my dread
of mortuary things, the biered casket,
painted corpse, rosary entwined

among the fingers of the folded hands,
the kneeler, placed a bit too close for comfort,
floral wreaths, standing guard on either
side like scarlet-coated sentinels,
kinfolk asking, "Who are you again?"
the priest's stinking breath and shaving cut—
I packed an overnight and for the next
three days, I stayed close to Maeve,
at her mother's house, the funeral home,
in the church, by the open grave.

I'd never seen her weep before, not
like this, so hard I thought she'd break. And yet
her laughter seemed to come from just as deep,
rushing off to welcome old friends of
her father, looking at forgotten photos,
thumbing souvenirs, serving coffee.

Every moment had its glut of feeling,
rivulets that fed a swollen stream
that drew and repelled me equally.
This was not the Maeve I thought I knew—
underneath that nickel surface there
were depths unseen, unthought and unsurmised.
Like oil on leather, pain had sweetened her.

Sunday night, the bones buried, guests
away, dishes done, food put up,
we talked in the doorway for an hour
or more, her voice, hoarse from overuse,
a distant look in her brimming eyes,

an unfamiliar smile that haunted me.
She laid her fingers on my arm and put
her head against my chest and her body
shook. I held her face between my hands
and kissed her eyes before I said goodbye.

Driving home in the dark and rain, I almost
turned around. You're going the wrong way,
I told myself. Wherever she is, that's
the place where you should be, where you belong.

She stayed with her mother for a while.
I didn't see her, but at night lay dreaming
of my Vasilisa, Frog-Princess.

Was it nothing, just a fantasy?
Did I make it up? She came home
the same old Maeve she was before the tears.
The other woman, she who had my heart
from the funeral was gone. I looked
for her in vain.

          A door slammed at my back,
I heard the deadbolt, didn't turn around.
Her sorrow opened me to love
but when it passed—ah, me—I lost them both.

vi.

They let the night nurse go, finally,
but not because of what she did to me—
that would be too much to expect.

Neck tats, buzz-cut, third-eye piercing,
I never liked the woman anyway.
She finished up her crossword book and knowing
that I slept with my newspaper
underneath my pillow, stole it in
the night.

I found it sitting in the trash
and when I showed it to the senior nurse,
Ms Brady of the burgundy pajamas
gave her standard answer—wait till ten
and bring it up in group therapy,
as if some other patient in the unit
was to blame.

I stayed calm, enough
to sidestep the needle, but I stood
my ground and I wouldn't let it go.
"Suppose somebody took the stethoscope
around your neck while you were napping?"
She agreed to let me see the doctor.

In a rumpled white coat with his name
embroidered in blue thread, Dr Tubbs

was staring at the chart in front of him
(it wasn't mine) when I came in the room.

He didn't hear a word of my complaint,
but offered up his own boilerplate—
for him to do his job, I must be honest,
above all, and I must promise I
would never try to harm myself again.

"I've said before, that was a mistake."

In the looney bin outside outside these walls
there was no *why* and no *because,*
so downing pills and chasing them with vodka
added up.

       Before it all went black
it came to me—some biologists,
I had read, could map an entire
species from a single specimen.

So why not designate a single day,
(since every one's exactly like the last)
and dissect it, fix it to a slide,
put it underneath a microscope?

I held the paper up with my finger
on the masthead pointing to the date,
how many months ago, when the aide
wheeled me through those metal doors into
a room the colors gray and chlorine

and I sat there waiting for someone
to draw my blood and take my vital signs
and confiscate my belt and my shoes.

I shook the pages. "Here, if I look deep,
is everything I need to explain
everything. This is holy writ."

Turning on to page five, I said,
"See here, a man shoots his wife in
the head. They don't say why, they never do,
but the answer's there if you think—
he was petrified of losing her."

From the front page, column upper left:
"Fighter pilots rain white phosphorus
and two-ton bombs down upon a people
with no air force. 'Self-defense!' the leaders
cry, calling fire on women, children,
hospitals, even cemeteries—ghosts
of enemies will terrorize the nation."

In the middle of the second section:
"Earth's a raisin, drying on a celestial
vine, food for intergalactic ants.
We shut our eyes with our fingertips,
afraid to peek, lest we be afraid.

I'm convinced that the line that threads
them all is this—we exit from the womb,
screaming, not in pain but in panic,

and even if the lucky ones are soothed,
it is too late—the moment has already
left its mark. We emerge, all
of us, from head to foot, tattooed with fear."

Dr Tubbs was silent, then he said,
"Whaddya expect me to do about it?"

"Tell your goddam nurse, it's *my* paper."

vii.

The drought had remained with us so long it seemed
a thing distinct unto itself, rather than
the absence of a thing. The crops of humans withered
in the field, their cattle fell and rotted where
they stood.

             Our pond home was shrinking by the day,
the black circle pulling tighter like a noose.
We all knew the time was not that far removed
when the sharp-taloned birds drowsing on
the dead white limbs of the surrounding trees
would wake to easy pickings in the shallow water.

The bigger fish hovered at the muddy bottom
with the snails and the scavengers, crowding
smaller fish to the surface where the ravens,
with a watchful eye for any flash of silver,
swooping down, snatched them up and bore them off.

I didn't worry that the birds would come for me—
being a newt, my rough brown skin is poisonous.
I have no enemies (except a certain snake
with long yellow stripes, occasionally spots).

Normally I wandered where and as I pleased,
through various lands, investigating sundry species,
but the world beyond this puddle was a desert
and for me to leave just then would not be smart.

Of the fish, the best and most beautiful,
eyes aglow like rubies, rainbows glinting off
the scales in the angled shafts of murky light,
Bodhi, they called him, or her, I wasn't sure,
was sick at heart and wept, if a fish could weep.

"The remaining days of this my family
are measured out in droplets that dissolve in air,
never to return." (Bodhi had a somewhat
ceremonious style, but I kind of liked it,
found it interesting.) "The time has come to spend
the virtue I've been saving, for my righteousness
to satisfy a larger plan. I will entreat
Pajjuna, son of Devagabha. 'O Great One,'
I will cry, 'why do you hoard the silver waters
that should flow to these? Release them, let them fall
where they are needed.' Pajjuna knows that I am good—
for my sake alone, he will save us all."

"Are you mad?" I said. "Have you lost your mind?
You put so much as a fin above the water,
birds will dance upon your back. The time is short—
are you in a rush to die?"

                    "Nevertheless."

Bodhi ascended listlessly, like one already
dead, through the limpid dome, and as a master
to a servant standing by:

Bring the flash
bring the thunder
bring the rain
save them O Pajjuna

An osprey turned its yellow eye and raised its beak,
and pushing off, it oared the air with monstrous wings.

The swish of fins and tail lifted Bodhi higher
in the water, and even louder than before,
he called out to the thundercloud deity.

Talons, black and cambered like the crescent moon
pierced the glistening scales and the high-and-mighty
raptor rose in flight with Bodhi in its clutch.

I watched till it became a dot on the horizon,
and with legs folded, thrusting with my tail,
I burrowed in the bottom mud to meditate.

I couldn't see the sense of Bodhi's sacrifice.
What did it achieve? One less wolfish bird
in the trees, one less fish in the pond.

I fell asleep and was awakened by a tremor
in the earth. Above, the sky was puffy black.
Lighting struck, scattering the hungry birds.
Drops began to fall in twos, fours, eights, sixteens.

Pajjuna is a fraud, I thought. He turns a blind
eye while Bodhi's taken, then decides to send

the rain, after all? Ridiculous. No—
god or no god, either way, the rain would come.

And yet the fish huddled close at the bottom
where they genuflected in thanksgiving for
the elevation of their Bodhi into heaven.

viii.

My shrink had had enough, my portraits on the walls
of his shoebox office with the leather chair
for him, for me, the couch with Kleenex on the arm.

He meant my dad, depicted as Attila Hun,
a Flemish merchant bearing scales and bag of gold,
dying on a pillow, hairless, skeletal,

my younger brother as the Prodigal returned,
eyeing with a grin the liquor and the women
at yet another celebration in his honor,

my former wives portrayed in pastoral scenes as Laban's
headstrong daughters, one of whom I hated
and the other loved, trouble either way,

charcoal studies of ex-girlfriends turning up,
a teacher with her hair in Nazi rune barrettes,
a boss with burning eyes in a Gorgon face.

Old Doc Freud said I should put them all away,
curate another exhibition, long delayed,
on a subject I'd avoided up to now.

"Avoided? Her?" I said. "How I wish I could,
but the song keeps playing over in my head—
M is for the mound of shit she ga-a-ave me.

She's the thundercloud at every barbecue,
the oxidizing jaundice staining every prize,
the slug that kills the rose of every love affair.

They say the past isn't even past and people
sigh and roll their eyes, but for me it's just
another way to say she can't be truly dead

when at night she stirs a deadly potion in
my dreams, and her tongue spews out white phosphorus
that burns through all my wrappings down to skin."

And yet I knew the old trick-cyclist had a point—
for me to ever have a chance to free myself,
I had to bring her with me to the weekly couch.

I asked myself, had it always been like this
with us? Rummaging, I found a photograph
someone had given me at her funeral,

professionally done in a studio,
dry-mounted with the name of the photographer
etched in gold leaf on the bottom right,

expertly lit against a seamless muslin sheet
of gradient pastel without a trace of shadow—
Mom and me.

I'm maybe six months old, diapered, my cheeks
tinted artificially red, my chubby arms
extended for the toy in the assistant's hands.

Mom is dressed like Easter Sunday, jeweled bracelets,
pearls, a fox fur round her neck, her auburn curls
washed with a ruby tinge, the same as me.

Looking at it now, I couldn't help but notice,
Baader-Meinhof fashion, a thing or two
I never had before.

The glow of young motherhood is contradicted
by a smile that seems more grimace-like the more
I stare at it.

She holds me on one knee, as far from her lap
as she can manage, no madonna here—
any farther out there, I'd be on the floor.

And yet another story's told in the eyes—
What am I doing here? they say. Please, dear God,
somebody, save me, give me back my life.

Here was all the evidence. I didn't need
to burrow any deeper. At last I had the truth—
from the start, my mother was my enemy.

I dreamed she stood before me. I held out my arms
to her and they turned to plastic yellow tape
stamped in black, POLICE LINE DO NOT CROSS.

I woke, and apropos of what, I didn't know,
it came to me, I had it wrong, just the reverse—
from the start, I was *her* enemy.

ix.

Ladies and gentlemen of the jury,
the following summation will be brief.
The Lord is my attorney, speaking through me,
and He utters not a word too much.

The facts are these: a gang of boys assaulted
me, mocked my ministry and God.
My bears escaped their cage and punished them.

The prosecution holds me liable for
the suffering my animals inflicted.
It's up to you, the jury, to decide,
first, was the crime committed by
myself, or Somebody else? And then,
was it in fact a crime and not just due?

I will commence by reminding you,
as the prosecution has allowed,
the ownership of bears by private persons
in this state is not against the law.

I found them, abandoned in the woods,
two cubs without a sow. I rescued them,
gave them names, Judith and Jael,
and built a chain-link pen to be their home.

They grew up hulking, powerful and fierce.
When I would come to feed them they would rise
up on their haunches, yet I had no fear—
my faith was as David's when he smote

the bear that seized a lamb from his flock.

The prophet Amos says, the Day of the Lord
will come and it will be as if a man
escaped the lion just to meet the bear.
Hosea preached that God would chastise Ephraim
like a she-bear sheltering her cubs.
Daniel prophesied the coming war
against the Bear, Russia, bringing forth
the Antichrist and the Rapture after.

The prosecution calls the victims,
my tormentors, children, but that's false.
You heard me call them boys when I said
they held up God Himself to ridicule,
but they were more than that—young men, in fact.

Mine is a humble wildwood church
on pilings in the shade of sycamores
with milky leaves from the dust of trucks
up and down the unpaved road in front.
The paint is peeling from the clapboard sides,
the steeple is of tin, the bell long gone,
the pews, raw pine, just like the floor.
I'm neither reverend nor minister,
just what they call an old country preacher.

The church isn't far from my house
and I used to walk there, past the rust-stained
mobile home where two or three of these
immoral youths resided with a woman

who earned her bread as Jephthah's mother did.
Red-haired, nearly naked, tattooed like
a daughter of Moab, she would sit
out in her yard in a folding chair
and when I passed her on the road, laughing,
she would beckon me to sin with her.

And then her young men and their friends
would trail behind me like a pack of savage
dogs, till they grew tired of the game.
They thought to shame the Lord by shaming me,
His messenger.

                On the day in question,
these youths pursued me home, into my yard,
throwing taunts, dirt clods, dogshit, (pardon
me, I call it what it is) and rocks.

As you know, the prosecution has
accused me of unfastening the gate
to release the bears, but I did no
such thing. I was nowhere near the cage,
as several of the boys have testified.

In evidence, the state's attorney offers
up the fact, admitted by myself,
that I called down a curse on those young men.
It's true. I didn't argue or complain
or compromise. I placed them in God's hands
and asked for Him to do with them as they
deserved.

And when the Lord brought forth His judgment
I did not object. The ones who died
had trespassed far beyond redemption.

Was it His own hand that raised the latch,
or did He guide their claws? Either way,
it was His Will, as everything that happens
is from Him.

I am aware that some
may find this hard, but to know the Lord
is to know, His ways are not our ways—
the Flood, Sodom, Lot's wife turned to salt,
the holy slaughter of the Canaanites,
King David's census, the sufferings of Job,
the Gates of Hell for all eternity.

When I took the stand, I laid my hand
upon the Book and swore, "So help me, God."
These attorneys swore upon the Lord
when admitted to the bar—the judge,
when appointed to the bench.

And you,
ladies and gentlemen of the jury,
took this pledge when you agreed to serve.

If you believe what you said, you must
believe that God was righteous to avenge me
(though I do not matter) and Himself
through malice of the bears—for what man will

accuse the Lord of Hosts of doing wrong?
You then must cast your ballot to acquit.

But if you don't believe, why did you swear?
Like all deeds without faith, your oath is worthless,
hollow words, mere talk—and who
are you to stand in judgement over me?

x.

The summer I was twelve, two friends
and I were hanging in the park
and Billy Dane came over, said
he had something he wanted us to see.

He was older, a couple of years
at least, and we thought he was
a little strange, but with nothing
else to do that August day,
the three of us followed him
into the shed behind his house,
atilt in two directions,
the windows fogged and veined with dirt,
the air inside mephitic from
manure, mold and rancid gasoline.

He leaned against the workbench, facing
us all gathered round and said
to watch and do the same as him,
unbuckling and pulling down
his trousers to his knees, and loosened
from the swaddling underwear,
it popped up like a jack-in-the-box
when the crank rises to
the highest note and quivered in
the air like a backseat bobblehead.

The three of us stood and stared,

then one, I don't remember which,
started to unbuckle his,
and not to be left out, I did the same.

Mine was standing too (it would
do this at the oddest times)
and I thought about the game
I used to play in the tub
when I was maybe five—walk
the bouncing board with two fingers,
spring up when I reached the end
absurdly high and then dive
head first into the tepid, soapy water.

Billy demonstrated with
a shuttle motion I had never
seen, nor even thought about.
Curious, I did the same,
and the rising ecstasy
pushed me past the point of no return.

Walking home, it came to me,
this was what the Boy Scout handbook
meant when it said on page
four-oh-eight there was a thing
that no *real boy* would ever do.
The book was vague on the act,
but clear in its denunciation.

Late that night in bed I made
a teepee with one knee so that

my brother wouldn't see and I
repeated the experiment again.

An ocean wave came crashing down
on me and when it ebbed, it left
a jagged, dripping rock of shame—
and nothing since would ever be the same.

xi.

Racewalking to my car, out by the chainlink fence
topped with razor coils of concertina wire,
the air itself seemed frozen and my windpipe ached
despite the cashmere swaddling my nose and mouth.

Six weeks since the solstice, leaving work at five,
underneath a sky the sallowest of blues
full of leaden gray, pink-bottomed clouds,
my eyes never deviated from my steps—
my summer troubles had solidified, just like
the mounds of black ice I skirted on the walk.

We'd capsized so many times I'd lost count,
still I took for granted that our little boat
would right itself on its desultory course—
it always had before.

                              But in July she came,
asking for a separation—not a word
about divorce, yet I went there in my head
and tumbled headlong into shame and self-loathing.

August brought the kiss-and-makeup getaway,
a week in a rented cottage in North Truro,
paid for months ago while we were still together.
Days we danced antipodal around the stone,
nights she would withdraw to the other bedroom,
and I would contemplate the light beneath her door

as she stayed up late, writing to a lover.

September, the truth emerged and her boyfriend
bolted. We could put aside the past, I said,
but she doubled-down and moved in with a friend.

I once was masterful at being by myself
but my self-reliant self had atrophied
like the muscles of a casted broken arm.
I ran before and after work to exhaust
myself, but the moment I turned out the light
my thoughts forked in threads running parallel.
I forgot to eat and drank too much when I
went out with friends to keep from going home.

October came, we tried again, a country inn.
For me it was a hoped for kindling of hope,
for her, a test to see if I could make her feel
the feelings she once used to feel, the way that movies,
TV shows and anthems on the radio
convinced her that she ought to feel. I failed.

With nights growing colder, we spoke scarcer on
the phone and when I went to see her I was held
at elbows' length. Over Christmas holidays
I had a brief affair which only made things worse.

With all this heavy laden on my mind, I set
out for my car that bitter day in February.

Coming to the bridge across the drainage ditch

which carried runoff through the corporate compound under
Boston Avenue, I heard a high-pitched wail,
too biting for a passing ambo or police.

A dog, brindled black-and-orange with a white
muzzle and no collar, had fallen in the ditch,
running back and forth, shrieking like the damned,
its paws breaking through the papery ice into
the shallow, running stream below at every step.

Now and then the stray would gather all its might
and vault against the concrete wall to reach the top,
but it was too high and the dog would fall
back on its haunches with a smoky howl.

I jogged across the bridge and down a narrow path
through the weeds to the rim of the canal.
The wall this side was lower and I whistled, slapped
my thighs, and called out, "Here, boy, come on, over here."
He turned to me and sprang into the air, landing
thirty feet away, clinging to the concrete
edge, but he couldn't hold—his nails slid off
before I could get to him. He tried again,
another place, again I came too late.

The dog's strength was ebbing lower every time—
soon he'd have none left and night was coming on.

I took off my overcoat, my scarf and gloves,
stuffed my tie into my shirt, and stood atop
the rampart wall. The dog sprang up, and this time I

was close enough. There wasn't much to grab but when
I wrapped my fingers round his toes, they held fast.
I pulled and the dog was on the wall.

                                        He shook
himself and disappeared into the winter weeds.
"Go on," I cried, "why should you be any different?"

My hands were covered with a gummy stuff like tar
from the mongrel's feet (why they didn't slip).

I closed my eyes and stretched my arms above my head,
offering my pitch-smeared palms to the sky
for deliverance.

xii.

The Brothers Louvin, Everly, and Righteous,
Simon and Garfunkel, Hall and Oates,
Loggins and Messina, Air Supply—
Gary and me were gonna be the next.

Sunday mornings in the Baptist band
I played guitar and G was on the keys.
They'd let us take the microphone and sing
the songs that we had written with the lyrics
modified to magnify the Lord,
but in return we had to hunker down
behind the sermon, suffocating yawns
and lacking straws to prop up falling eyelids.

At sixteen, I did mostly as I pleased,
but Gary's parents trimmed his feathers close
and every place was branded out-of-bounds
except the church. Still it was a hive
of people coming, going, all week long—
we just had to show up and someone
would stamp our hands with an alibi.
Gary learned to disconnect the speedo
cable on his dad's old Pontiac
so they couldn't tell how far we drove,
and we were free to raise equal hell
with the unredeemed. And Baptist girls,
not all were virginal—some had read
their *Genesis* and gathered what it means

in saying Jacob goes in unto Rachel.

It wasn't only G and me—the crowd
of us they called "kids" were edging the
Abyss, or so the elders, prizing youth
as gold, believed. To save us from ourselves,
they dug a pitfall, baited with the beach.

I took my guitar and G and me
sang for fishers, volleyballers, bathers,
eyes peeled for the surf-untied bikini.

The day was setting and with recompense
still to be made, they herded us to face
the Preacher. Not much older than we were,
his theme was as old as Augustine—
two young men, best friends for all,
one dying with his soul defiantly
his own and handed over to immortal
pain, becomes a warning to the other—
his doom could just as well be yours.

In the press of gathering dark, the Witness
stretched his arms and flamelets of Hell
rose from where the thumbs and fingers joined.
He preached as if he'd toured and taken notes:
"Hellfire is the Death that follows death.
Some say you die to oblivion—
preposterous, unbelievable.
Some say Hell is like a prison sentence—
idiots, it doesn't end, ever.

Some say it's wrong the Lord would invent
a place like that, but He is perfect justice—
the burning lake, slakeless thirst, worms
that never get enough of human flesh,
are exactly what we bargained for.
All well and good, I say, if you're afraid—
we Christians ought to twitch in holy fear."

By now, his mouth a torch of swirling fire
like the muzzle of artillery,
all around they're rising, shuffling zombie
feet toward the Gospeler to drop
their green teenage sins and batten on
the pap of ransom, once withheld, now paid.

I never felt so cold inside, colder
than the sulfur of Beelzebub
was ever hot. A snowman with his feet
in sand, I stood in arctic silence as
the rest joined hands and circled round a bonfire
singing praise—and with them was my friend,
his voice, sharper than the rest, and in
his eyes, a look that said, Depart from me.

xiii.

Since Munich, scarce a word—
I combed the itinerary, seeking grounds
to look across at her and speak.

"Turns out, we're on the Orient Express," I said.
She never heard of it.
"No? After we get off in Vienna,
it goes all the way to Istanbul.
Imagine if we stayed, kept on riding,
tried our luck among the Turks."

"They've done without for centuries.
So what about the train?"

"Well, it's famous, in a literary way, or used to be.
A stage for misfits, Graham Greene called it Stamboul Train.
Chasing Dracula, Van Helsing hypnotized Miss Harker in First Class.
Snowbound in Croatia, Hercule Poirot cracked a guild of
executioners."

"Fascinating."
"Never said it was. You asked."

Susan wore her book like a hooded cloak.
My focus dithered back and forth between
reflections in the window glass
and silhouetted trees in the dusk beyond.

Sometime after midnight
we put the seats together in the middle
and stretched out head to toe.
"Like Molly Bloom and Poldy."
"Who?"

I coveted her sleep—
insomnia held the door
for succubi of memory.

Last April, I got leave, stateside for a month.
One night together led to every single,
and with my sands declining toward the shank,
afraid to say goodbye, we wed in mutual clutch.

June, she flew to Germany
to live with me as man and wife
my last summer as a soldier,
soon to be civilianized.

Home from duty in the afternoon,
tired and hot and sticky,
we would cool down in the bath
and ignite in bed.

July, a day submerged in sun, we biked to Würzburg—
rolling seas of hills with rafts of old-growth trees,
fields with scattered coils of hay, taller than a man,
villages steaming with manure and rancid Pilsner,
distant towers crowned with cobalt onion domes.

We stopped to pick the chicory beside the road
and watch a disc of sheep glide slowly cross a hill,
the shepherd trailing mindless in processional steps,
his dog encircling the flock against the dial,
a fermata in the music of time.

But after that the gears began to come ungeared,
the cogs uncogged, springs sprung, the chain unchained.
Her discontent pooled in airless darkness where no candle burned,
her talk became a litany of things she didn't want,
chief among, to sleep with me.

Vienna!
Excess of excess,
fountainhead of *gemütlichkeit*,
bridesmaid city of the Habsburgs,
Paris with a Balkan smell,
whose streets taught Hitler how to hate—
as a boy I rhymed it with hyena.

In my roster of penurious hotels
I found a nest of crumbling walls
around a center court.

Our host, Hungarian in Italian knit,
a nose to match his pointed shoes,
bragged of gypsy blood.

His wife, an eye faint yellow-green,
a week from black,
handed me the register and my change.

Past noon, not long before the day would start to sag,
I bounded up the stairs to stow our luggage in the room,
and as I hurried past,
like a conference of birds,
a clutch of women in the hallway,
barefoot, in many-colored wraps,
turned their sleepy heads to chirp at me.

The taxi driver asked if we were tourists
and we returned indulgent smiles.
Planning this since she arrived,
choosing artists,
sequencing museums,
fingernailing maps,
we didn't need a docent.

'We've come for the Secessionists," I said.
Actually, my wife had come
as I had promised.
Her thesis almost done,
interviewing paintings in the flesh
would clinch her case.

In a round of portraits at the Belvedere there were no males—
this artist painted none but women.
But I had an eye—
I could tell he'd fucked them all.

To see their magic gowns,
decorated in goldleaf

and crazy-quilted hues,
celestial iconography eclipsing scandal,
I thought about those off-duty ladies
idling in the hall,
who made fun of me.

They were there when we returned
and more, a line in front of the hotel
in sequins shimmering like sockeye scales,
aureole to prat.

In the hall upstairs a man came through a door
and swung his tie up into the notch.
He called out to his friend just starting down the steps,
Lukas, warte auf mich!

"Did you know?" she asked me from the bed.
I said I should have but I didn't think.

Had I ever been a place like this before?
I said no, but once, in truth, I almost did.
It occurred to me, the merchandise
would have a smell, a taste, a voice, ideas,
and I left the store.

"So what now?" she smiled. "When in Rome?"

We lay in spoons on the narrow bed.
The worm eating at my heart for weeks was strangely still.
I was happy, hopeful everything would be—
all right.

I thought about my father.
Mornings, when I lived at home,
now and then he'd be like this—
it was almost possible to live with him
if he'd spent the night in my mother's bed.

What saith Buckingham?
O, let me think on Hastings, and be gone.

I heard again the man to Lukas on the stairs, "Wait for me!"
Maybe they were still around,
in the bar across the street,
on the sidewalk waiting for a third,
considering how next to use the night.

Get up, get up and follow, go and find them.

Lying there, I thought about it for a while,
until it came to me, I would—
if not for love.

xiv.

God said to Moses in the wilderness of Meribah,
Speak to the rock and the rock will bring forth water.

I'd seen it on TV, in the movies, on the stage—
somebody in a cemetery, talking to a block
of granite, fused, it seems, with the sleeping dust below.
In monologue to the dead, the actor makes his speech
and cleansing always follows.

                     I admit, it was a case
of Life aping Art, and I'd have laughed at anybody else.
But do we always have to know why we do such things?
Is apparent nonsense larded with a secret logic?

At any rate, it was something I had not yet tried,
and with the graveyard situated not far from the airport,
I could fly in, speak my piece, and out the same day.
Efficiency, if nothing else, argued in its favor.

I hadn't visited since the second burial
twenty years ago, me not even thirty yet.
Underneath the white sun of a steaming summer day
I drove the labyrinthine roads in a rental car,
looking for the site, and only found it when I saw
the stump, all that remained of the bygone live oak tree
that spread its benediction on those blackcloth funeral days.

The same year graven on both halves of the memorial
didn't tell the story, how they died just months apart

of matching fatal cause, his and hers dependency,
my mother for the jar of sour mash, my dad for her,
a drug of potency impossible to quantify.

Carved in the upper right hand corner of the marker
(I could not remember whose idea—it wasn't mine)
an angel with a banner and the words in cursive hand,
Together Forever—

                    Punishment enough, I told myself.
Their dance upon this earth was infernal, hell in common.
If, as I roughly held (obviously I must,
or else I wouldn't be here now), the circle is unbroken,
at this moment they were somewhere, going through the steps.

Before I speak, I thought, I should capture their attention—
even ordinary times, no easy thing to do.
I saw a stick nearby and picked it up and rapped the stone.
I laughed, thinking how it hadn't worked for Moses either.

The toes of my shoes nudged against the marker's foot
among the parched and withered uncut weeds. Two steps back,
I tried to speak and failed. I'd come a thousand miles to say
I wasn't angry anymore, but the words simmered
in my gut, my tongue was like a dried-up watercourse.

("Angry? What about?" you ask, as I knew you would.
If I should litanize their lunacies, you'd lean forward
with your chin between your hands saying, "Tell me more,"
but if I bared the cicatrices in my milquetoast heart,
old lesions oozing still, you would yawn and turn the page.)

It seemed to happen overnight—one day I looked,
resentment had enough, my constant knocking at his door
with therapeutic zeal, always querying his rights
and wishing he would leave. He packed his bags, decamped elsewhere.

The room he occupied was empty now, the windows crusted,
papers on the floor, empty hangers in the closet,
so I thought, it was only right to let them know.
No longer enemies, perhaps they'd visit now and then.

But my intentions turned to clotted ash inside my mouth
that oven afternoon as I stood there by the grave,
feeling nothing, either way. Not a lack of *something*,
rather *nothing*, positive, entire, autonomous,
miles of nothing, acres, heaps, years, dollars, reams,
a flood of nothing, nothing but a teacup in my hand.

I retreated, stepping crab-like side-to-side in arcs,
each one more distant from the axis of the stone.

I reached the safety of the car and took an early flight,
the clean cathartic bite of vodka-tonic on my tongue.

XV.

Erect, cool, proud, though manacled,
his seamless robe bloodsoaked in the back,
bloody streaks dried upon his face,
tapped out from a long sleepless night,
watching the clepsydra with one eye—

I see it like a film in black-and-white,
Rod Steiger in the role of Pontius Pilate.
Who plays the crucified? I can't decide.
Jesus is too legion for one actor.

He answers cryptically, defiantly,
as the procurator's questions rate,
and startles with a swift parting shot—
he has come to witness to the Truth.

For the first time Pilate lifts his head.
"So tell me, what is—," he spits out the word
like a bite of gristle in the meat, "—*truth?*"

Socrates, four hundred years before,
sat on a bed with a cup of hemlock
and provided Plato with enough
material for three whole dialogues.
From Jesus, not so much as a nutshell.

Rockefeller said, you inquire
about my yacht, it means you can't afford it.

There seems that sort of arrogance in Jesus'
silence, as if saying without words,
You have to ask, you wouldn't understand.

Pilate's query's mockery—he is
a Pyrrhonist, a ratifier of
the Jersey-barriered axiom declaring
truth unknowable and life only
livable when you call off the search.

There was a time when I thought more like that
than not, before defecting to the other
side, where instead of equals zero
truth is myriad—a sky of stars
about their business on a winter night,
a sanctuary, populated with
too many beasts for me to keep them straight,
a crumbling mansion, home to ghosts
that flutter in and out like bats.

       I'm tired.
I'm feeling with my foot for the single path.

Three years he walked the land with his disciples,
Nazareth to Jerusalem,
speaking parables to camouflage
his meaning from the spiritually unwashed,
like me.

   Now here's his chance to tell it straight.
So what, if I don't understand?

Why can't he say it anyway? What
would be the harm? What is there to lose?
Let me be, to gather what I can
from the stubbled border of the field.

Jesus' stance is plumb, in cross-armed silence.

xvi.

A Christmas stereo
meant my own music, my own room,
headhones, my own time.

The catch? Albums cost.
After school in the record store
I looked at cover art, pondered liner notes and left.

When I did have money
I could spend an hour pulling ten from the racks
to cull a half a dozen must-haves,

winnow achingly to three necessities,
on a hunch or eenie-meenie-meinie-moe
crown one or two at most.

Beethoven, Brahms, a desert-island pick.
Rossini made me laugh out loud,
Tchaikovsky made me weep.

Ammons, Blakey, Coltrane,
Dolphy, Hancock, Miles—
look for the oval on the front,

Baez, Dylan, Ochs,
PPM, van Ronk,
simplicity and truth,

Aretha, Chubby, Drifters,
Junior Walker, Marvin,
Otis Redding, feed my soul with Stax.

Of course The Beatles,
minus mania—
not even Mozart was *that* good.

I held my breath
as I dropped the needle,
side one, band one, something new,

but it cost a fortune to keep up
and sans the public library I might have been
propelled into a life of crime.

Someone told me they had albums
and I snubbed it as a rumor—
Monte Cristo was a fantasy.

Yet there they were, upright in bins,
alphabetical, within genre,
like the store.

Now that I could walk away
with four or five or six at the cost of air,
I took chances, branched out, courted unfamiliarity,

which is how I happened on Chicago blues—
five guys in front of some outlandish shop
that sold incense and herbs,

all dressed differently in gritty urban styles
(bands wore uniforms!)
and two of them were Black.

I turned the jacket over for the exegesis
and in unbelief I had to read it twice,
the warning near the bottom:

TO BE PROPERLY APPRECIATED THIS RECORD MUST BE PLAYED AS
LOUD AS POSSIBLE

I'd never had the gain past noon—
it felt unsafe,
like urging Dad's old Ford into the red.

The sidebar with its turnabout of rules,
like the Tower card dealt horizontally,
portended something ominous.

I didn't know it yet but I was living on the eve,
when not just music, all of life
would become "as loud as possible."

Brit-bands, folkies, sweet soul music
drowned by Hendrix,
Zeppelin and Sabbath,

domestic wars over length of hair,
state of dress,
opinions,

smoke of giddy laughter
rising to a frenzy of amphetamines,
lysergic acid, heroin,

so many hopes dissolved
in Memphis and Los Angeles,
the paddies and the highlands of Vietnam.

I foresaw none of this,
yet as I read the words I must have sensed
a tremor from the future aslant time

because I put the record back,
went home and put on Brahms—
good ol' Brahms.

xvii.

The orchestra pit is a kind of ditch
where they hide musicians from
the glitterati in the seats sublime
down front. Above, in the mezzanine
and balconies, ballet-lovers are
subjected to a galaxy of glowing
music stands whose superfluity
illumines twenty seesaw fiddle bows
and sometimes flashes from a silver flute
or the golden bell of a trombone.

Down in the pit, behind the cello squad,
I couldn't see the *assemblé, sauté,*
jeté, the *temps levé,* but I could hear
the thump of satin-slippered ballet feet
and sense the lighting's vacillating moods.

The score was bright and airy, cotton candy
music, cloying as champagne, threadbare
on its own *sans bijou* of dance—
face-melting, heavy metal guitar
would almost be a welcome interlude.

I looked forward to my sixty-four
bars tacet in the middle of Act Three,
when Nureyev himself would withdraw
aside to the apron of the stage
in perfect view of me, five feet below—

Basilio, the wily barber who
outfoxes old Lorenzo and Gamache
to marry his beloved Kitri watches
lesser dancers dancing at his wedding.

Each performance, I would stare impaled,
once so rapt I almost missed my entrance.
Every time I thought, if I could get
a sub for one performance I would pay
the scalper's fee and never mind the cost.
If he could show panoptic standing there,
what must it be like to see him dance?

Afterward, as I left the hall
I'd see him standing by his dressing room,
the torso of a comic superhero
in a t-shirt baggy as the sacks
his Bashkir forebears used to lug potatoes
from Siberian fields, his thick Tatar
hair tucked underneath a crazily
outsized newsboy cap with studded bling.

Pilgrims lined up serpentine awaiting
compostela. Eyes too ponderous
to lift, he signed the tendered playbills with
a Sharpie flourish, dead illegible.

He made me think about balloons the next
morning after last night's celebration,
or a mill on strike, early Monday
in the church, the beach in January,

a hollow gourd, the bread you throw to birds,
a flower pressed in an antique book.

I could see that in this man it was
no common, ordinary weariness.
Whatever let him do what he could do,
he had bartered all to get this far.
If I met him on the street just now
I wouldn't know him and I'd turn away.

Musicians, dancers, passed me, talking, laughing,
tripping out the door with evening plans.

Only the *danseur noble* in the funny hat,
who didn't look so funny, seemed to have
nowhere to go and nothing else to do
but stand with empty pockets, offering
his steadfast devotees a hand of crumb.

It was time for me to leave, myself.
I had done my job, to play the notes,
a part deserving of my instrument,
if nothing more—plenty in my cup.

Which is why no one paid me the least
attention as I ducked into the night,
a mind of footling thoughts akin to shame.

xviii.

Summertime and I was six years old,
playing with Alicia, the girl who lived
across the street from me, also six,
her hair long and straight, in a jersey
dress, tennis shoes, ankle length
white socks trimmed with eyelet lace.

Sitting in the grass, she was threading
clover stems while I was searching for
the whistle hidden in a blade of grass.

I asked if she knew how to do a cartwheel
and I took three running steps, fell forward
on my hands and folded in the middle,
finished lying on my back.

"You're doing it all wrong," she said.

                              I watched
her heels orbit in a perfect line.
She landed on her feet with a *ta-da!*

I was glad no other kids were there.
To see her dress fall down around her waist,
they would laugh and sing, "I see London,
I see France," and she would turn to beet
and dart away inside to her mother.

She wheeled again the other way and I
was hushed by the glow of cotton white
in the liberal sun of summer morning.

The garage behind my house was old and gray,
tumbledown, unused for anything.
The door was sagging from a broken hinge,
and it took all my strength to open it
enough for us to squeeze inside.

In the light bleeding through the slatted
walls I could see the dirt floor had been raked
and how our footprints squashed the furrows flat.

"I go," she whispered, and I followed her
to the corner farthest from the door.
Her hands disappeared beneath her dress,
the cotton white came down upon her shoes,
she draped the skirt from her bellybutton.

Adam seeing Eve the first time
could not have been more mesmerized than me.
"Could this," he must have asked in wide-eyed stare,
"could it be, *this* is Eden, not the garden?"

I'd never heard of Eden. I had no name
to fling against, to temper or subdue,
the spell that held me there, the why unknown.

I fell to one knee in the dirt.
Alicia giggled, did a little dance

with her feet in jubilation
as serendipitous to her as me.

I put out my hand, not to touch—
I couldn't—but to shield my eyes against
the piping splendor of a nakedness
that made my belly buzz with honeybees.

Unseen fingers snaked into my hair,
curled to claws, and yanked me on my back.

I raised my head, Alicia wasn't there—
she had escaped. It was my mother in
the corner, eyeing fury down on me.

She hauled me by the elbow to the kitchen
steps and stopped to wrench a branch, almost
as long as I was tall, from the hedge.

I watched her strip the leaves and then I felt
the fire on the skin below my knees,
the Flaming Sword of Eden turning every
way to ban lovers from their home.

xix.

The woman on my left, tendering
a diamond hand and a Gail Somebody,
asked me how I knew the birthday girl.

"I don't," I said.

            She cocked her head as if
to wonder, had I seeped into the crowd,
been washed in here to dinner uninvited?

I pointed to my wife, head to head
with the guest of honor at the far end of
the table, segmented like an arthropod
underneath the long white linen cloth.
"Old college roommates," I said.

She chattered like a magpie, twenty questions,
but I didn't take offense. At least
she primed the pump with something of her own
for every cup she tried to draw from me.
I learned she was a lawyer with two children,
married to a chief executive.
She'd grown up in the South, now was living
in New York.

          "Me too," I said—like her
I was a Dixieland expatriate.

"No!" she cried aloud at the name
of my hometown. "That's where I was born!"

"No!" I cried at the neighborhood.
We held up birthdays to the light, the years
the same, Virgo her, Pisces me.
"I lived there, first and second grade
in the red brick building with the porticos
and the glass on Peachtree Battle Ave."

"The school! Oh yes." She clapped her hands for joy.
"I had such a crush on Jeffrey Johns.
Me and April Harms and Amy Smith
ate lunch together every single day.
And Mrs Emmons—you remember her,
the sweetest thing that ever walked the earth."

She searched my face for an amen. I shrugged
and smiled like a thief caught in the act.

"Miss Mack?" she tried again. "Played piano?
Taught us all those silly songs? No?
Mr Martin with his magic tricks?
Miss Dobbs, the Principal? What I'd give
to have that woman at my daughter's school."

She reviewed the evidence as if she had
the archive of her childhood, indexed and
cross-referenced, lying open on the table.

I listened in astonished silence to

so many names from so long ago,
each one as unremembered to me now
(or erased) as my name was for her—
she had no memory of me at all.

She did her best, I told her so, and
apologized for drawing blank. She smiled
and turned away to introduce herself
to the person sitting on her left.

I tipped the amber ice and closed my eyes
and remnants of the place and time appeared
like patches on a sable velvet curtain.

Jeffrey Johns—was it him who shoved me
in the cafeteria, splashing
me with boiling chicken noodle soup?
All that afternoon I stank and burned
and counted up the blisters on my hand.

April, Amy, Gail—weren't they
the ones who laughed and said to go away
when I put down my tray too close to them?

Emmons, Mack, Martin, Dobbs? I called
my own by different names.

                    The Ugly One
of desperate midnight hair, a moly face
sculpted out of Crisco, needled like
the Holy Spirit, God gave me a brain

and I tempted Him with idleness.

The Fat One, a barrel with pickup-stix for legs,
called me Christmas, since I did it slow,
like my grandfather, and they all laughed.

In the palace of the Wicked Queen,
it was treasonous to raise your hand
and I saw the spreading pool of yellow piss
underneath the girl in front of me.

.

Recess I would run to the dog trail
through the bushes by the fence and stay there
till the bell, always the last inside.

Someone touched my arm, the woman Gail:
"The waiter needs to know what you want."

I said the fish and turned to her to ask
if she'd like to talk some more about
the school. "It was years ago," I said,
"but now—I think it's coming back to me."

XX.

Finally I remembered—*Old Man Reynolds.*

I'd been at my desk, for half an hour
at least trying to recall the name
of the man who owned the house and woods
across from me before I moved away.

The old man was a great lover of birds,
or at least a great keeper of them
in a long, low coop of cinder block
with a little pond for the swans.

All day the chickens clucked and scratched,
the pigeons came and went, flights of doves
murmurated aerobatically,
guinea hens, louder than a textile
mill, flocked about the neighborhood,
digging into people's flower beds,
in mating season, peacocks—or peahens,
I wasn't sure—yelped like city sirens.

Complaining was no use—Bethel had
no jurisdiction there across the road
and Danbury refused to entertain
a plea from someone not a resident.

Sitting solitary in my empty
office, nothing there for me to do,

random thoughts of birds and other useless
information drifting through my head—
such was my everyday, ever since
I got the early morning call
advising me that there had been a meeting
and my job had been eliminated.

A veteran of corporate bloodletting,
controlled burns of so-called staff reduction,
I should have seen it coming, but to work
from home is to find yourself outside
the pale of office politics, which
is where the early warning signs appear.
The way my doom so took me by surprise
showed how marginal I had become.

I started sweeping papers from my desk
into the trash, moving personal files
from the corporate laptop to a thumb drive.
My final day was curiously busy—
a last expense report to complete,
the severance agreement to review
and decide about insurances—
health, life, disability,
accidental death/dismemberment—
the money in my 401K,
escrowed in my stock purchase plan.
I packed the company gear up in a box,
any way it would go, and took it
to the nearest FedEx dropoff point—
and that was that.

Now what? I wasn't like a painter
staring at a vacant canvas or
a writer at an empty sheet of paper.
They had some idea—I had none.

Each morning I got up the usual time,
made the coffee and buttered a bialy,
and guided there like runoff to a rill,
I padded to my desk and breakfasted
exactly as I had the past two years.

The phone the firm no longer paid for
wasn't going to ring. I had no screen
to read, no inbox to prioritize—
my email address had been scrubbed
and messages to me were bouncing back.

Yet I would sit there half the day, my mind
on burning issues like—whatever happened
to Old Man Reynolds and his stupid birds?

One day, without warning, they were gone—
nobody seemed to know just where or why.
Perhaps he'd grown as tired of them as the
rest of us, or some citizen
of Danbury had at last complained.

He tore down the coop and drained the pond,
filled it in with earth unmounded flat.
Of all the flocks there remained a single

swan and every time it rained the bird
would waddle cross the grass to the tiny
puddle where its ocean used to be
and plop down with its proud black head aloft.

In my mind I could see that swan,
the rain beating on its snow-white plumes,
its arching neck more exquisite than
the quilled flourish of an antique hand,
squatting in an inch of muddy water.

My God, I thought, that's me—I'm that swam.

The Women

To Robert Alter

A*bigail*

A widow now—it's a miracle
Nabal survived the week, his doctors said.
They thought at first he wouldn't last the night.

The nurse held my hand and sighed. I breathed
my first easy breath in seven years,
since I married him.

                    Nabal's sister's
going around, saying I murdered him.
I only did what I had to do.

The restaurant was jammed with customers,
enjoying free champagne, menu discounts,
cornhole for the kids, a live band.

I knew the three of them were David's men.
There was that bulge underneath the arm,
plus I remembered one from last year.

"Congratulations on your tenth year
in business," they said to Nabal.
"Voted Best in the Borough, featured
on TV—you're doing very well.
Be a shame if there wasn't an eleventh."

Nabal was drunk. "You come here with a threat?"

"Easy now, you'll spoil the celebration.
We can see you're busy. We'll be brief.
Remember the *mattanza* a year ago,
the war with those crazy fucks from Philly?
Thanks to David, you had our protection,
day and night. We surrounded you
like a wall—just ask your people, they will
tell you. All the time, the restaurant
stayed open, in addition to your more,
let's say, profitable businesses.
You didn't lose a dime. So now's your chance
to pay it back. We count on you to give—
it's in your interests to be generous."

"A lot has changed in the last year,"
Nabal said, "but one thing hasn't—Saul
is still the Boss. And David? Who the fuck.
is David? An outlaw on the run, that's all.

One of the men reached for his nine,
another laid a hand on his arm.

"Saul loved him, made him," said Nabal,
"even had him as his son-in-law.
But David never learned, you don't outshine
the man who raised you up where you are.
If Saul wants him gone, that's up to him.
Who am I to say otherwise?
If I get mixed up in this, I am dead.
Tell your captain, he can go to hell."

(86)

The men whirled away and left without
another word. Nabal watched them go
and stumbled off, looking for a game.

Christian came to me, his face like bone.
"I know David's crew—my cousin's one
of them—and they won't hesitate.
They're coming back, tonight, and in numbers,
I'm afraid—tell us what to do."

I stopped the party, closed the restaurant,
had the cooks fill up the catering truck
with food and top-shelf liquor, all the best.
Christian drove and they followed us.

I met David coming out the door.
My voice trembled as I said to him,
"This is all my fault—if I had known,
I wouldn't send them off empty-handed."

He was in a rage, refused to listen.
"I never killed a woman but I've made
my share of widows. Nabal's a walking corpse,
and anybody who opposes me."

I took one step closer, then another.
"My so-called husband is a dried-up thorn
in everybody's side, a yolkless egg,
a coin of no value stamped in tin,
a tick engorged with blood that's not his own—
your enemies should all be just like him.

But he has powerful connections
and you will need them, when they make you Boss."

David put his hand across my mouth.
"Shut up! I said to Saul a hundred times,
I'd no desire for any honor he
was not prepared to give, but because
of careless talk like that, he wouldn't
take me at my word, and now I'm living
with the consequences."

                    David's crew
surrounded us, armed and primed. The wires
to a dozen hearts lay in his hands.

I smiled and opened up the truck so they
could see the steaks, the ribs, the lamb, the lobster,
while my cooks got down to business.

I took off my coat, still in my evening
gown, so David could enjoy the gift
I brought for him.

              "Nabal isn't stupid
like I thought," he said, and took me by the hand
to lead me off.

             "He doesn't know I'm here.
I did all this. It was my idea."

"I bow to you, madame. Your husband doesn't

understand how fortunate he is."

I caught Nabal in the morning, sober.
"You don't know how close you came last night.
It doesn't matter what you think of David,
he's a fact. If you want to stay
alive, I suggest you give him what he wants."

His diamond ring left blood on my cheek,
not for the first time. I made up my mind,
it would be the last.

        "That's not all,"
I said. "I spent last night as David's queen.
He praised me for my beauty and my mind
and all the whorish ways you trained me in
since I was not much more than a girl."

A corner of his mouth began to droop,
he groped the air as if he couldn't see,
tried to get up from his seat and fell.
He might have called my name but it came out
gibberish.

        David phoned a while
ago, offering condolences.
He said he'd be around, in all day.

I'm due at the funeral home and then,
if anybody asks, that's where I'll be.

Michal

He wouldn't come under the umbrella.
He stood bareheaded in the freezing rain.

He reached for me, I pushed his hand away.
"Abner's by the car, watching us."

He pleaded for me not to go with him.

"You knew it could come to this and now
it has. You talk as if I have a choice."

"But I love you—what else can I say?"

"Nothing," and I laughed in bitterness.
"You love me, I love David. I don't
love you, David has no love for me.
The magnet ends are all misaligned—
as if that matters up against the rest."

The death of Saul my father led to open
war with David. Then my cousin's halfwit
insolence left Abner, Papa's loyal
second-in-command, without a choice
aside from standing down with all his men.
Now peace was in the air and as my father's
only remaining child, I was the key.

"Mikki is my wife," David said.

"Give her back, we can end this now.
But until you do, look for blood."

And switching sides, Abner came for me
himself, which meant that David would be Boss.

I kissed my stand-in husband on the eyes
and on the mouth, the way he did to me
at goodbye, and turned and walked away.

He came behind, weeping like a child.
Abner fronted him and opened up
his coat to show the nine beneath his arm.
"Turn around," he said. He hung his head
and walked back to the house.

                        In the car
I kept my eyes closed until the squish
of tires in the mud turned to sizzle
on the wet blacktop.

                    Abner wondered
how I'd stood it here, so far outside
the city, any life. "I'd go nuts.
Your boyfriend ain't what I would call a man."

"No, not what you would call," I said.

Abner wasn't much himself these days.
The years had knocked him around, plenty—
rheumy-eyed, jowly, purple-nosed.

And David? I hadn't seen him for so long.
The only thing I had was an old
photograph, the one the agents flashed
when they came to the door, a lovely face
that even a mustache would sabotage.

We hid our love, afternoons out
of town or staying over at my friend's.
Papa wanted David for my sister,
perfect, quiet, docile, sweet and kind.
"No, sir, I don't deserve her," David fawned.
"I don't deserve to be your son-in-law,
but with Mikki, I'll be satisfied."

Beside me down the aisle, my father muttered,
"*Due traditori*—which one's worse?"

He was thinking of the ditzy women
in the bars singing drunken songs
to David's fame, or how the crews admired
him for his courage, and because
he was too shrewd and smart to run his mouth.
Jonathan, my handsome, now dead brother
was in love (though David never knew),
and Papa loved him too, nights he couldn't
sleep, when David sang his songs for him.

From a handful spores of jealousy,
carrion flowers of hate multiplied.
Papa wanted David dead, but while

they lay in wait for him outside, I helped him
to escape, under their very nose.
So I deserve my place at David's side.
If not for me, they would have taken him
for a ride and he'd be just a name.

He has others (I know all about
the woman with the husband, had a stroke)
and though I am a marker in his game,
a trophy, passed from hand to hand and back,
I'm not sad to go to him. I am
who I was and he is who he was—
some part of who we were must still remain.

Bathsheba

Baba tries to make it all my fault.
I meant no harm. I tried to help, is all.

Yuri had been gone for weeks, down south
where David sent him, and my sister wasn't good
at being by herself. Besides, she
was still a bride—a month to go until
her first anniversary. But David
didn't give the wives a second thought
and Yuri did whatever he was told.

I read about it in a magazine—
maybe if she sexted him, I thought,
reminded him of what he had at home.

He messaged not to do it anymore—
he had a job to do and that came first.
He was the man and she should shut her mouth.

I said to Baba, "Go nuclear—
a video." My roommate studied film,
had everything we'd need.

          It was Baba's
choice to do it at the titty bar
where she worked when she and Yuri met.
Her former boss said we could have it to
ourselves in the morning before lunch.

"I forgot how much I like to dance,"
Baba said, "but I'm so out of practice.
A blister from the pole already—get
my purse so I can break it with a needle.
This halter hangs on me like a sack.
How'd I ever move in shoes like these?"

I'd never seen her do her act before—
she wouldn't let me, said I was too young.
At home, she was always the pretty one,
but never so alluring as today.
Baba wasn't taking off her clothes,
Baba was constructing fantasies
in thin air with movement, light and shadow,
mimicking the catalog of love
and promising it all with eyes that never
wandered from the lens. She closed the set
in a pair of pleasers, nothing else,
walked up to the camera and said,
"Yuri, baby, this is just for you."

Yuri took a day and flew back home.
He was in a rage and he smacked
her around, a bit, but not that much.
She was stung mainly in her pride.
It was wrong, but he did it out
of love. The soldiers laughed at him because
he didn't have a *comare* on the side—
he was just as faithful to his Baba
as he was to David and the crews.

One night I found her dressing to go out.
Some dress—crêpe-de-chine with an
open back, plunge in front, split to
the thigh. David sent it to her door,
and then he sent a car.

                       He lived alone,
with nobody but his bodyguard.
Nights his limo pulled up stealthily
in front and when I heard about the kid
I knew at once it wasn't Yuri's.

David summoned Yuri home, they talked
a little business, drank some Cutty Sark,
and then he said, "I can see you're tired.
I won't keep you any longer. Go on
home to that gorgeous wife of yours."

"He knows," Baba whispered. Yuri wouldn't
sleep with her, not so much as stay
the night. He hardly spoke. "With David, he
pretends, plays it cool, but with me—"

David sent him back to Florida,
and one week after that he was killed.
Nobody talks about it, but to ask
why Yuri took on Scarpa by himself.
Where was his crew? Why weren't they with him?

Baba gave a lavish funeral

and everybody came. Now she's living
in a condo in Astoria.
David's there sometimes, mostly not.
I'm only welcome if she feels like it.
She knows I know it wasn't any of
the soldiers sent the video to David.

Her baby died—a birth defect, they said.
She just had another boy. Both
of them are doing fine, so I hear.

A*bishag*

My Aunt Lucia called, "Come for tea."

I was surprised to find my uncle there.
He was so rarely home. He turned to me
a buttered smile and said he needed help.
I didn't know what to say—it wasn't
like the man to ask.

               He said the Boss
was still the Boss, but he was getting on.
Days, David was his usual self
but nights in bed he could not get warm,
no matter how they raised the thermostat,
how many blankets they put over him.
The chill radiated from within
and the covers only made it worse.
They needed someone young and lovely, like me,
to lie beside the Boss at night, unclothed.

I laughed. "That's all?"

                   "Strictly for the warmth,"
Aunt Lucia said. If the man could not
perform, nakedness was innocent.

I said okay and took the job. The money
was too good—that was how they did.

At first it was as if I wasn't there.
He lay on his back, mummy-like,
his muscles taut as a crouching cat.
I touched him on the arm, a shiver like
a bolt of lightning racked him head to foot.
I stretched out and pressed against his side,
my arm across his middle like a rope,
and bit by bit he settled into easy
sleeping breaths, long, longer, deep.

Aunt Lucia had it right when she said
I might just as well be a teddy bear.
He never asked my name and in the dark
I wasn't certain if he understood
it was the same woman every time.

And when the chill at last would dissipate
he would lie there, singing songs he'd written
long before I was even born
in a voice like a withered apple,
words so beautiful I asked myself,
who is this man? Not the one he seems.

One night I couldn't sleep. I rose and lit
a scented candle, sandalwood and fig.

"Turn around," he said, "so I can see."

I bowed my head, bending at the waist,
my hand between my breasts, Geisha-like,
lambada-ed to the mirror hanging on

the door, the two of me in perfect time,
crept across the quilt and once again
the shriveled voice arose:

> You are my dove
> my purest one
> bright as the moon
> brilliant as the sun

He put his left hand underneath my head,
his right against the small of my back
and he washed over me like ocean waves.

The moment came much sooner than I thought—
my charms against the cold ceased to work.

Despair wrested him from my arms.
"I never thought I would end like this—
I waited for a bullet for so long.
Is there a man I killed I would not
again? Then why is it I feel as though
it was all a waste of desperation?"

He took a sudden turn, they moved him to
a home. Afternoons I would come
to sit beside the bed and hold his hand.

Once he mixed me up with someone else.
"Baba says I promised I would name
her son to take my place when I am gone.
Did I say I would? Do you recall?

I'm not sure. I forgot. If Baba
says, I guess so, but his brothers
will be angry—he's the youngest son."

Not so, I would have told him if I could.
Your youngest son is here inside of me.
If she knew I carried David's child,
Baba would have us killed.

                              I was in
a corner of the room when David passed.
Abigail wept into her hands,
Mikki looked on, wordlessly, in
her eyes, the sugar-glaze of fentanyl.
Baba didn't stay—she had what
she wanted, even if there'd be a war.

I gathered up the envelopes,
bellied at the seams, that David left
beneath my pillow, took a red-eye to
the other coast, drove north along the shore
until I found a cabin by the sea
in a hollow where the fog comes rolling
every night, and hidden from their eyes
my child was born.

          Now every day I sing
to my sweet David and I watch him grow.

www.ingramcontent.com/pod-product-compliance
Lightning Source LLC
Chambersburg PA
CBHW020755130626
46554CB00006B/2195